Towards the Source

from *Poems (1913)*

Christopher Brennan

Introduced by David Brooks

ETT IMPRINT
Exile Bay

Published in Imprint Classics by ETT Imprint, Exile Bay 2026

First published as *XXI Poems: Towards the Source* by Angus & Robertson 1897. Revised and reprinted within *Poems (1913)*, Angus & Robertson 1992.

ETT IMPRINT
PO Box R1906
Royal Exchange NSW 1225
Australia

ISBN 978-1-923527-22-5 (paper)
ISBN 978-1-923527-40-9 (ebook)

Cover: Christopher, woodcut by Lionel Lindsay
Cover and design by Tom Thompson

A Sydney-Paris Link publication
in memory of Jean-Paul Delamotte

TOWARDS THE SOURCE

Christopher Brennan, an etching by Lionel Lindsay.

Introduction

On October 5, 1932, there died in Lewisham Hospital, Sydney, a huge man whose great, leonine mane of black hair falling over the pillows framed a handsome face dominated by an eagle nose.
An impressive-looking man, you would have said. Alive he had "fascinated several generations of students" at Sydney University and "dominated all the artistic and bohemian circles that mattered in the Sydney of the early twentieth century."

Lionel Lindsay[1]

Christopher John Brennan was born on 1st November 1870 at home in Harbour Street, the Haymarket, Sydney and died on 5th October 1932, just three weeks shy of his sixty-second birthday. His Irish father, also named Christopher, from County Kildare, had trained at the Guinness brewery in Dublin. He'd come to the colony in 1864 and was now brewer at the Castlemaine Brewery on nearby Hay Street. Christopher John's mother, also Irish (County Tipperary), was Mary Ann Carroll. Christopher was - would become - the eldest of five surviving children.

Although his father might have disagreed with the Sydney Catholic hierarchy on the matter of temperance, Brennan's family was staunchly Catholic. Christopher attended local Catholic schools and for a time seemed intended for the priesthood. At the age of ten he was the sole acolyte at the Good Samaritan School on Pitt Street, and in the year following attended the Jesuit St Aloysius College, where he first encountered the poetry of John Milton, who would leave a life-long impression. Three years later, with a bursary extended by Cardinal Moran, he began to attend the newly founded St Ignatius' College, across the harbour at Riverview, as a boarder.

Brennan did not become a priest. 'Religion began to worry me', he wrote in an unpublished autobiography (henceforth *Curriculum vitae* (*CV*)[2], 'in my nineteenth year: it seemed to me that I lacked fervour, that I was mechanically repeating a dull exercise.' In 1888, at the age of seventeen, he began to attend the University of Sydney, initially to study Classics but increasingly drawn to Philosophy, his religious impulse now transformed into an attempt, evident in so much of his poetry thereafter, 'to elaborate a special epistemology of the Unknowable, which was also the Absolute.'(*CV*) Upon his graduation in 1891 with first-class honours and a University gold medal he took up, briefly, a teaching post at St Patrick's College in Goulburn, where he wrote his first serious poetry (and seems to have had a brief love-affair), and in 1892, awarded the James King of Irrawang Travelling Scholarship, went to Germany to study at the University of Berlin.

At the University of Sydney he had become, in Axel Clark's words[3], 'passionately attached' to the poetry of Tennyson and Swinbourne. In Berlin, purchasing that poet's remarkable *Vers et Prose* (1893), he encountered a further and much deeper influence in the poetry of Stéphane Mallarmé. In large part under Mallarmé's influence, as Clark details, 'he decided to "go in" for verse: for the next ten years it became the most important thing in his life'[4]. Poetry, that is, and Anna Elisabeth Werth (1870-1948), the beautiful daughter of his Berlin landlady, with whom (Anna Elisabeth) he had fallen in love and to whom, against her mother's wishes, he had become betrothed. Perhaps owing to the combined distractions of poetry and Anna Elisabeth, his Berlin studies did not produce a degree.

Brennan returned to Sydney in 1894. Anna Elisabeth (he would call her Elisabeth) did not join him until 1897. The reasons for this separation are not clear. They may have had to do with Frau Werth's disapproval; they may have been financial. Australia was at this point in the midst of an economic depression. Although he was given some part-time teaching, Brennan did not return, as he might have expected, to an academic position. His principal occupation was instead in the New South Wales State Library, which remained his primary employer until 1908, when he at last gained a University of Sydney appointment. This is not to suggest that this period was unproductive. 'Brennan's early love poetry,' as Lionel Lindsay would later write, 'written after his return to Australia and before his bride-to-be followed him, witnesses to the intense love with which the marriage opened'[5] – so much so, in fact, that in 1899 his nomination for a full-time position at the University of Sydney was vetoed by the chancellor and vice-chancellor because of what they saw as the immorality of some of his verse.

Christopher and Elisabeth married on December 18th 1897 in St Mary's Cathedral, on Hyde Park. For a time they appear to have been happy. Their first child, Anne, was born in 1898, their second, Elisabeth, in 1901. Some growing tensions between them – in several ways they were very different people – were not aided by Frau Werth's arrival in December 1900, 'with a deranged daughter' (Julie, Elisabeth's older sister), to join the household, nor, we might presume, by the fact that Frau Werth arrived with financial resources such that Brennan would find himself henceforth materially obliged to someone who disliked and disapproved of him. 'Slowly', writes Clark, for these and other reasons, 'Brennan's marriage began to drift towards disaster'[6].

The family at this point settled in Mosman, into a house Frau Werth had had built upon one of several blocks of land she had purchased. Two sons, Christopher and Rudolf, were born here, in 1906 and 1907 respectively. In 1903, according to Guy Jennings[7] Brennan (but was it in fact Frau Werth?) bought a four-acre plot at Newport, as a weekend retreat, and built two cottages there. Evidently this retreat, 'on a slope overlooking the beaches and headlands that extend to Barrenjoey', gave the Brennan family some pleasure. His daughters, for example, were in 1910 part of what was reportedly the first girls' beach life-saving club in the world. But the outbreak of war in 1914, and Elisabeth and her mother's emphatic support of Germany, added a severe burden to the already troubled relationship, as one must imagine did the rebellion of Anne, its eldest child, who in 1917 was convicted in the Children's Court, banished from the household lest she influence the rest of the children, and eventually (albeit briefly) turned to prostitution.

Brennan was at last, in 1921, promoted to associate professorship in German and Comparative Literature at the University of Sydney, seemingly consolidating his already-established reputation as 'one of the most profound scholars of European literature, ancient and modern that Sydney University has ever known'[8]. This appointment might have brought him some satisfaction but it does not appear to have brought much calm to his marriage. He soon (1922) left Elisabeth and formed, with Violet Singer ('Vie'), a divorcee eighteen years his junior, a relationship which brought him some joy at last and became the source of a number of his most fondly-remembered poems. In March 1925, however, just three months before he would find himself dismissed from his university post for adultery, Vie was killed by a late-night tram. 'Her death', writes Clark, 'had a terrible effect on Brennan. Crushed in misery, he aged overnight, and looked a broken man.'[9] Although there were some brief periods of respite (a period in 1927 teaching at the Marist Brothers' High School in Darlinghurst; a 'sustenance fund' established by friends; a pension, in 1930, of £1 per week from the Commonwealth), his life thereafter – a life, as some at the time and many have subsequently said, of one of Australia's finest, if also most troubled and perplexing poets – disintegrated into alcoholism and isolation. And in 1932 cancer brought an early end to it.

There were only three commercially-published volumes of Brennan's poetry in his lifetime. At the age of twenty-three, upon his discovery of the work of Mallarmé, he had vowed to destroy all the poetry he'd written up to that point. One or two early poems may have nevertheless survived, but in essence his first collection, printed in eight copies only, *XVIII Poems: Being the first collection of verse and prose* (1897), was very much in Mallarmé's shadow, albeit underpinned by the heat of Brennan's first passion for Elisabeth. In the same year, hot on its heels, Angus & Robertson published *XXI Poems: MDCCCXCIII-MDCCCXCVII,* subtitled *Towards the Source.* Two hundred copies were printed. Most of them remained unsold. Although Brennan was deeply disappointed by the book's almost complete failure to draw public attention, he cannot (or perhaps should not) have been greatly surprised. Self-consciously intellectual, oblique, laden with strange terms and references, it stood stubbornly against the bush balladry that characterised do much of the Australian poetry of its time

Although Brennan had written some extraordinary work in the interim (e.g. *Lilith,* concerning the legendary first wife of Adam but doubtless motivated in part by his own marriage difficulties, and *The Wanderer,* with its Nietzschean undertow), no second collection appeared until *Poems* (now generally referred to as *Poems (1913*) - in 1914.

This volume began with an expanded version of *Towards the Source*. Much of the rest was written between 1897 and 1904 or in the three years (1911-13) before its appearance.

A fourth collection, *The Chant of Doom and other verses*, was published in 1918. This, Brennan's only commercial success, comprised poems written in the previous four years in what he'd come to see as a regretful and misguided attempt to help the war effort.

A fifth collection, *The Burden of Tyre: XV Poems* – 'an attack on England and Australia … for their aggression in the Transvaal' during the Boer War – remained unpublished during Brennan's lifetime. Composed in 1903, this might have appeared as his third collection, between *XXI Poems* and *Poems (1913)*, but was withheld by him, supposedly for 'its strong anti-British sentiment' (G.A. Wilkes)[10], and save for a few handwritten copies would not appear until a private edition by Harry F. Chaplin in 1953.

Accounts suggest that, in the eight years between composing the bulk of *Poems* in 1897-1903 and completing the project in 1911-13, Brennan seemed depressed, and to have somehow lost his way. Doubtless the causes were in some part biographical. Brennan was mid-life (he'd turn forty in 1910) and mid-career, and that career had experienced, in 1908, a significant and doubtless demanding change with his university appointment. His household, already strained and crowded by the arrival of Frau Werth and her troubled elder daughter, had become all the more so with the birth of his second daughter in 1901, and of his sons in 1906 and 1907. One can imagine that in such a situation something had to give, and that that might have been his poetry, particularly after the disappointing reception of *XXI Poems*.

It might also be that he'd experienced a blockage inherent in the poetry itself. Mallarmé had held out, to the poet discovering him in the early 1890s, the possibility of an Absolute – a kind of return to a lost Eden – but even Mallarmé seems to have come, by 1897, to a realisation that, attractive spiritually and philosophically as this prospect might have seemed, it was also illusory, impossible. His *Un Coup de Dés* (1897), revolutionary a poem as it was in form, presents its situation as a shipwreck, the ship's master somehow imprisoned and impotent in the debris. It may be that Brennan, in this 'lost' period, had come to some similar point, and to a kind of loss of faith in his project.

The problem might also have been structural. Along with Mallarmé's *Vers et Prose* had come, for Brennan, the concepts of the *livre composé* (composed book), and of the *Grand Œuvre* (great work) – in essence the notion that a book (in this case of poetry) might at one and the same time be itself a composition or construction rather than a collection of miscellaneous pieces, and part of a larger composition or construction of work beyond it (and perhaps of one's life's work). It is possible, that is, to see Brennan's trajectory as having begun, enthusiastically, upon such a project in *XXI Poems (Towards the Source)* and continued in that direction for a few years afterward, but then as having encountered structural and conceptual problems, or perhaps a loss of faith in himself and the project, that slowed or halted his progress for a period of years before, resolving them, he found the further inspiration to return to the project in the four years leading up to *Poems (1913)*.

It might also have been aesthetic in a broader sense. Brennan was not only trying to create, in *Poems (1913)* and perhaps beyond them, a Mallarméan construction but also, over the period in which he did so, trying to negotiate, stylistically, a passage or transition into a new century. Other poets were endeavouring to do the same thing. In the English language WB Yeats (for example) was struggling to shift his register from that of *The Wind Among the Reeds* (1899) to the more direct, 'realistic' language of *The Wild Swans at Coole* (1917), Rainer Maria Rilke, in German, was struggling to shift his register from *The Book of Hours* to that of his remarkable *New Poems* of 1907. And Ezra Pound was casting about for ways to shift his style from that of *A Lume Spento* (1908) to that of *Lustra* (1916). If Brennan's 'The Wanderer' evokes Nietzsche's Zarathustra, for example, it also evokes the Old English Exeter Book's powerful and lonely lament of the same name and invites fruitful comparison to Pound's revivification, in *Ripostes*, of its companion Exeter Book poem, 'The Seafarer'. That Pound's Exeter Book-based portrait of the poet-as-lonely sailor, cast out of Eden, forced to embark (Odysseus-like) upon an arduous journey/voyage into the unknown (the new century), so like Brennan's wanderer – comes ten years *after* Brennan's, might give us a clearer sense of Brennan's achievement. Perhaps Brennan, in this sense, was a little too much ahead of his time, and that time, when it came, never went back to collect him.

Although there are, amongst his poems, some striking exceptions, in general Brennan's transition did not get so far as some of these other poets. On the other side of the world (as it were), he had his own additional handicaps. The distance itself, for example, from what were then perceived as the cultural centres (London, Paris) and the 'cultural cringe' that can attend it. The fact that he was attempting, more or less alone, to establish an intellectual and philosophical poetry in a country much more comfortable with bush balladry. The fact that, whether or not he could maintain the faith per se (he did, in his last years, return to it), he was of a religious minority (Catholic) deeply attuned to religious symbolism, in a country not so attuned (he was predisposed, in this sense, to *understand* Baudelaire and Mallarme and the *symbolisme* they espoused, but also, perhaps, to cling to it to a point where it might trouble his readers, or simply fail to attract any.

But now to approach *Towards the Source* more directly. In his *Curriculum vitae* Brennan remembers the church of St Francis, which his family attended, and at which, in his eighth or ninth year, he served as acolyte:

> *On Sunday evenings in summer during Vespers, as the light waned, I used to watch the colours fade out of the window, until the body of the Cruxified turned livid grey, then for a while the leads stood out in a thicker black on the gathering dark. Next, the blaze of candles lit for the Benediction and the placing of the burse. The burse is of no use during the service: it has of course the same colours as the cope. These were, for the groundwork a dull light-absorbing gold, for the cross of the burse and the cape of the cope a deep ruby. I could never gaze on them enough: so the thrill when the burse was set up.*

It's a passage worth noting. It can be seen as containing the seeds or groundwork of a whole aesthetic. The window, and the light through it. The 'light-absorbing gold'. The 'cross of the burse and the cape of the cope a dark ruby'. Catholic symbols, yes, but I think the weight here is just as much on the power of symbols, *per se*, and of the words – the language – which carry them. Not only is 'the *cross* of the *burse* and the *cape* of the *cope* a dark ruby' a line of pure poetry, but each one of its items – cross, burse, cape, cope – is itself both a symbol and a word of some strangeness. A modern-day Catholic (and I am not one) may know some of these terms or items but I suspect many would have to look up one or more of them. We have thus, in this passage, a glimpse of the mystery of items, the significance of colour, and the love *and strangeness* of language, and poetry, itself. Things – and terms – are not merely themselves, but lead us to (contain, allow, usher through) other things, as the dying light through the window, say, changes and brings to life ('a *livid grey*') the body of the Cruxified. Brennan may have lost his belief in the God of his religion – become convinced that that God either does not exist or has become discredited, redundant – but the mystery of earthly existence, the sense that it is deeply imbued with something out there, beyond, that seems to promise us meaning, is all the keener therefore.

The window was a key locus for the Symbolist poets, from Rimbaud's *Les Chercheuses de poux* ('The Ladies who Look for Lice') to Mallarmé's *Les Fenêtres* ('The Windows'), symbolising the presence or arrival of light from elsewhere (the Source, the Absolute) to change or illuminate things of this world.

Towards the Source can be seen as a kind of extended *envoi*, at once a setting-out – we are embarking upon the *livre composé*, the composed book – and an introduction to the place or situation that book is setting out from . In this sense it begins in disillusionment – all its references to a lost Eden, to being cast out, to one's being now condemned to a kind of lonely exile – but there is, within this, a kind of paradoxical hopefulness, as if, an *illusion* having been lost, there might now be hope of finding a firmer, truer platform for one's understandings and aspirations. One Eden may be gone, but there are signs – experiences, moments in one's being – of the existence of another, toward which one might somehow find one's way. One of the concerns of *Toward the Source* is to present us with some of these signs and experiences that lead Brennan to think this might be possible, some of the evidence he feels there is, the God-illusion having been set aside, to believe there is some other Source or Absolute which draws us.

Most of the poems in *Toward the Source* are love poems, poems of the passion and exhilaration of love itself – the way it can seem to elevate one above the normal state of one's being, the way it can be taken as evidence that there is something beyond one's normal state of being. While love, significantly idealised, may dominate this part of the wider composition, Brennan readily acknowledges, and employs, other forms of evidence of the Absolute, other things that gesture toward the Source. Art, too, attempts to bring out of its subjects something not otherwise apparent. Beauty lifts and leads and haunts us. Poetry – beauty and strangeness within language – seems to seek to demonstrate that there are rhythms and rhymes within and between things beyond their initial appearances. And music. All of these things – the beauty and sometimes terror of the natural world is another of them – that seem to gesture to a sense and meaning beyond the mundane senses and meanings we live by. Gestures, if you like, toward – symbols of – a source we might once have termed God but now, free of that illusion, are endeavouring to see and understand more clearly.

Brennan is regarded as a 'difficult' poet, an acquired taste. It's been suggested one must study him before one can like him. His diction is frequently antiquated, frequently arcane. Why couldn't he – or wouldn't he – write more clearly? But this, too, is a *symboliste* technique, or Brennan's version of the same: language drawing attention to itself as a set of symbolic objects, used to *bring strangeness* into his poems, to attain or preserve a sense of the mysterious, the unknown, the ulterior.

A note about the text. *Toward the Source* exists in two quite different forms, that is, there is the *Towards the Source* as it first appeared, in (and as) *XXI Poems*, in 1897, and there is the *Towards the Source* as it appeared as part of the livre composé that is *Poems 1913*. For *Poems 1913*, Brennan dropped five of the poems that had appeared in *XXI Poems*, moved a sixth ('My heart was wandering') to *The Forest of Night* (the title he gave to the second part of his *livre composé*), and added fourteen poems that he had written or revised since. The initial, twenty-one poem version of 1897 had now become a twenty-nine poem version. *Towards the Source* as it is printed here is this 1913, twenty-nine poem version.

The five poems Brennan dropped from the 1897 version were 'First Nocturn (Northern)' ('I will free my soul from this stifling place'), 'Second Nocturn (Tropic)' ('Sighing—'), 'Bells' ('After the garish day'), 'Aubade' ('We woke together on a gusty dawn'), and '[Fatum]' ('Dumb Sibyl, sitting at my birth'). These poems have been added as an Appendix to this current edition.

The fourteen poems added to the 1913 version are 'Sweet silence after bells!', 'Epigraph (Black on the depths of blackest skies)', 'Under a sky of uncreated mud', 'Epigraph (A memory droops among the trees)', 'Where the poppy-banners flow', 'Was it the sun that broke my dream', 'When the spring mornings grew more long', 'An hour's respite; once more the heart may dream', 'Spring ripple of green along the way', 'I am shut out of mine own heart', 'Spring-breezes over the blue', 'Four springtimes lost: and in the fifth we stand', 'Old wonder flush'd the east anew', and 'The winter eve is clear and chill'.

David Brooks

1.'The Professor was a Poet', *The News* (Adelaide), 3 December 1954, p.26.
2. Brennan papers, Mitchell Library.
3. *Christopher Brennan*, Melbourne University Press, 1980.
4. Brennan entry, *Australian Dictionary of Biography.*
5. Op. cit.
6. *Australian Dictionary of Biography.*
7. *The Newport Story 1788-1988* (Aramo, 1987).
8. Lindsay, op. cit.
9. *Christopher Brennan: A Critical Biography* (Melbourne University Press, 1980), p.251.
10. Introduction to *Christopher Brennan: Selected Poems* (Angus & Robertson, 1973), p.viii.

TOWARDS THE SOURCE

1894-1897

MDCCCXCIII: a prelude

Sweet days of breaking light,
or yet the shadowy might
and blaze of starry strife
possees'd my life ;

sweet dawn of Beauty's day,
first hint and smiling play
of the compulsive force
that since my course

across the years obeys;
not tho' all earlier days
in me were buried, not
were ye forgot. –

The northern kingdom's dream,
prison'd in crystal gleam,
heard the pale flutes of spring,
her thin bells ring ;

the tranced maiden's eyes
open'd, a far surmise,
and heaven and meadows grew
a tender blue

of petal-hearts that keep
thro' their dark winter-sleep
true memory of delight,
a hidden light.

Then by her well Romance
waiting the fabled chance
dream'd all the forest-scene
in shifting green ;

and Melusina's gaze
lurk'd in the shadow'd glaze
of waters gliding still,
a witching ill ;

or lost Undine wept
where the hid streamlet crept,
to the dusk murmuring low
her silvery woe.

Dim breaths in the dim shade
of the romantic glade
told of the timid pain
that hearken'd, fain,

how Beauty came to save
the prison'd life and wave
above the famish'd lands
her healing hands

(Beauty, in hidden ways
walking, a leafy maze
with magic odour dim,
far on life's rim ;

Beauty, sweet pain to kiss,
Beauty, sharp pain to miss,
in sorrow or in joy
a dear annoy ;

Beauty, with waiting years
that bind the fount of tears
well-won if once her light
shine, before night).

Then the shy heart of youth
dared know its weening sooth,
then first thy godhead, Sun,
it's life's light one,

what time the hour outroll'd
its banner's blazon'd gold
and all the honey'd time
rang rich with rhyme –

rhyme, and the liquid laugh
of girlish spring, to quaff
granted each heart, and shed
about each head

a sound of harping blown
and airs of elfin tone
and gipsy waifs of song,
a dancing throng.

The yellow meads of May
acclaim'd the louder lay,
more rapturously athirst
for that fierce burst

of Summer's clarioning,
what time his fulgent wing
should cleave the crystal spell
his hot eyes tell

each charm beneath the veil
his eager hands assail
and his red lips be prest
against her breast,

filling her every vein
with the diviner pain
of life beyond all dream
burning, supreme –

(O natural ecstacy!
O highest grace, to be,
in every pulse to know
the Sungod's glow!)

Thence the exulting strain
sped onward as a rain
of gold-linked notes
from unseen throats,

till the mad heart, adust,
of August's aching lust
to do her beauty wrong
broke, and the song;

and in her poppied fate
keen life, grown all too great,
illumed with grateful breath
the lips of death. –

But these deep fibres hold
the season's mortal gold,
by silent alchemy
of soul set free,

and woven in vision'd shower
as each most secret hour
sheds the continuing bliss
in song or kiss. –

O poets I have loved
when in my soul first moved
desire to breathe in one
love, song and sun,

your pages that I turn,
your jewelled phrases burn
richly behind a haze
of golden days. –

And, O, ye golden days,
tho' since on stranger ways
to some undying war
the fatal star

of unseen Beauty draw
this soul, to occult law
obedient ever, not
are ye forgot.

1897

We sat entwined an hour or two together
(how long I know not) underneath pine-trees
that rustled ever in the soft spring weather
stirr'd by the sole suggestion of the breeze :

we sat and dreamt that strange hour out together
fill'd with the sundering silence of the seas:
the trees moan'd for us in the tender weather
we found no word to speak beneath those trees

but listen'd wondering to their dreamy dirges
sunder'd even then in voiceless misery ;
heard in their boughs the murmur of the surges
saw the far sky as curv'd above the sea.

That noon seem'd some forgotten afternoon,
cast out from Life, where Time might scarcely be :
our old love was but remember'd as some swoon ;
Sweet, I scarce thought of you nor you of me

but, lost in the vast, we watched the minutes hasting
into the deep that sunders friend from friend ;
spake not nor stirr'd but heard the murmurs wasting
into the silent distance without end :

so, whelm'd in that silence, seem'd to us as one
our hearts and all their desolate reverie,
the irresistible melancholy of the sun,
the irresistible sadness of the sea.

1894

Sweet silence after bells!
deep in the enamour'd ear
soft incantation dwells.

Filling the rapt still sphere
a liquid crystal swims,
precarious yet clear.

Those metal qui ring hymns
shaped ether so succinct :
a while, or it dislimns,

the silence, wanly prinkt
with forms of lingering notes,
inhabits, close, distinct ;

and night, the angel, floats
on wings of blessing spread
o'er all the gather'd cotes

where meditation, wed
with love, in gold-lit cells,
absorbs the heaven that shed

sweet silence after bells.

1913

Autumn: the year breathes dully towards its death,
beside its dying sacrificial fire ;
the dim world's middle-age of vain desire
is strangely troubled, waiting for the breath
that speaks the winter's welcome malison
to fix it in the unremembering sleep :
the silent woods brood o'er an anxious deep,
and in the faded sorrow of the sun,
I see my dreams' dead colours, one by one,
forth-conjur'd from their smouldering palaces,
fade slowly with the sigh of the passing year.
They wander not nor wring their hands nor weep,
discrown'd belated dreams! but in the drear
and lingering world we sit among the trees
and bow our heads as they, with frozen mouth,
looking, in ashen reverie, towards the clear
sad splendour of the winter of the far south.

1894

Where star-cold and the dread of space
in icy silence bind the main
I feel but vastness on my face,
I sit, a mere incurious brain,

under some outcast satellite,
some Thule of the universe,
upon the utter verge of night
frozen by some forgotten curse.

The ways are hidden from mine eyes
that brought me to this ghastly shore :
no embers in their depths arise
of suns I may have known of yore.

Somewhere I dream of tremulous flowers
and meadows fervent with appeal
far among fever'd human hours
whose pulses here I never feel :

that on my careless name afar
a voice is calling ever again
beneath some other wounded star
removed for ever from my ken :

vain fictions ! silence fills my ear,
the deep my gaze: I reek of nought,
as I have sat for ages here,
concentred in my brooding thought.

1894

Dies Dominica ! the sunshine burns
strong incense on the breathing fields of morn :
lucid, intense, all colour towards it yearns
that souls of flowers on the air are born.

What claustral joy to-day is on the air
– expanding now and one with the celebrant sun –
and fills with pointed flame all things aware,
all flowers and souls that sing-and I am one!

Dies Dominica ! the passion yearns,
and the whole world and singer is but one flower
from out whose luminous chalice odour burns
intenser toward the blue thro' this keen hour :

-this hour is my eternity! the soul
rises, expanding ever, with the sight,
thro' flowers and colours, and the visible whole
of beauty mingled in one dream of light.

1894

The grand cortege of glory and youth is gone
flaunt standards, and the flood of brazen tone :
I alone linger, a regretful guest,
here where the hostelry has crumbled down,
emptied of warmth and life, and the little town
lies cold and ruin'd, all its bravery done,
wind-blown, wind-blown, where not even dust may rest.
No cymbal-clash warms the chill air: the way
lies stretch'd beneath a slanting afternoon,
the which no piled pyres of the slaughter'd sun,
no silver sheen of eve shall follow : Day,
ta'en at the throat and choked, in the huge slum
0' the common world, shall fall across the coast,
yellow and bloodless, not a wound to boast.
But if this bare-blown waste refuse me home
and if the skies wither my vesper-flight,
'twere well to creep, or ever livid night
wrap the disquiet earth in horror, back
where the old church stands on our morning's track,
and in the iron-entrellis'd choir, among
rust tombs and blazons, where an isle of light
is bosom'd in the friendly gloom, devise
proud anthems in a long forgotten tongue :
so cozening youth's despair o'er joy that dies.

1895

Black on the depths of blackest skies
whence even the levin seems withdrawn,
the cities threaten : burning eyes
ask what dread hand hath slain the dawn.

Under a sky of uncreated mud
or sunk beneath the accursed streets, my life
is added up of cupboard-musty weeks
and ring'd about with walls of ugliness:
some narrow world of ever-streaming air.

My days of azure have forgotten me.

Nought stirs, in garret-chambers of my brain,
exept the squirming brood of miseries
older than memory, while, far out of sight
behind the dun blind of the rain, my dreams
of sun on leaves and waters drip thro' years
nor stir the slumbers of some sullen well,
beneath whose corpse-fed weeds I too shall sink.

1895

I

The yellow gas is fired from street to street
past rows of heartless homes and hearths unlit,
dead churches, and the unending pavement beat
by crowds – say rather, haggard shades that flit

round nightly haunts of their delusive dream,
where'er our paradisal instinct starves : –
till on the utmost post, its sinuous gleam
crawls in the oily water of the wharves ;

where Homer's sea loses his keen breath,
hemm'd what place rebellious piles were driven down –
the priestlike waters to this task condemn'd
to wash the roots of the inhuman town ! –

where fat and strange-eyed fish that never saw
the outer deep, broad halls of sapphire light,
glut in the city's draught each nameless maw:
– and there, wide-eyed unto the soulless night,

methinks a drown'd maid's face might fitly show
what we have slain, a life that had been free,
clean, large, nor thus tormented – even so
as are the skies, the salt winds and the sea.

Ay, we had saved our days and kept them whole,
to whom no part in our old joy remains,
had felt those bright winds sweeping thro' our soul
and all the keen sea tumbling in our veins,

had thrill'd to harps of sunrise, when the height
whitens, and dawn dissolves in virgin tears,
or caught, across the hush'd ambrosial night,
the choral music of the swinging spheres,

or drunk the silence if nought else – But no!
and from each rotting soul distil in dreams
a poison, o'er the old earth creeping slow,
that kills the flowers and curdles the live streams,

that taints the fresh breath of re-risen day
and reeks across the pale bewilder'd moon :
– shall we be cleans'd and how? I only pray, red
flame or deluge, may that end be soon !

II

Ah, who will give us back our long-lost innocence
and tremulous blue within the garden, else untrod
save by the angels' feet, where joys of childish sense
and twin-born hearts went up like morning-praise to God !

where we were one with all the glad sun-woven hours
and rapture of golden morn thrill'd thro' our blood and nerve:
– our souls knew nothing more than knew the unheeding flowers
nor their own beauty's law, nor what it was to serve.

But that dark lust to learn and suffer drove us forth:
we wearied of the light, of life unvaried, whole;
and seeking have we wandered, south and west and north,
some darker fire to fuse the full-grown sense with soul.

And see ! for ages have we dragg'd our long disease
o'er many a hideous street and mouldering sepulchres,
till not a capital of towers and blacken'd trees
but reeks with taint of us, drips with our blood and tears.

London or Tarshish, Rome and Paris our delights
have gilded and thereon have soil'd them: first and last,
flush'd with our wine and song, has shudder'd at our nights,
and cast us, lepers, out into the ancient waste.

Where grinning deserts hide unhid your skeleton stones,
Tadmor or Nineveh, our pomp has enter'd in :
the Dead Sea rolls more bitter above our blasted bones
and spews upon its shore the unwasted scurf of sin.

And what have we at last of all our wandering ?
the sadness of the flesh, the languor of the soil,
and this – hard eyes, scarr'd cheeks, lips that forget to sing :
– ah ! we could lay us down and let the deluge roll

our corpses into Lethe's pit – but that a breeze
has blown upon our eyes with tidings of the blue
still somewhere : let us bend this once our penitent knees,
then rise and seek for aye the garden that we knew.

Ay, let the cities pile themselves in the red mud,
and flare into the night that hides the offended heaven,
and belch their sodden dream of empire, lust and blood,
working in dread ferment of the old hellish leaven,

Psyche ! our feet are set towards the eastern star,
our eyes upon the spaces of the morning air;
what tho' the garden goal shine o'er sad seas afar,
tho' young hope guide us not, our soul shall not despair.

Enough, we shall have dream'd that solitary emprise,
enough, we shall have been true to our austere thought,
that, if we ne'er behold with longing human eyes
our paradise of yore, sister, we shall have sought.

III

Let us go down, the long dead night is done,
the dolorous incantation has been wrought ;
soul, let us go, the saving word is won,
down from the tower of our hermetic thought.

See – for the wonder glimmers in the gates,
eager to burst the soundless bars and grace
the wistful earth, that still in blindness waits,
perfect with suffering for her Lord's embrace.

The spaces of the waters of the dawn
are spiritual with our transfigured gaze ;
the intenser heights of morning, far withdrawn,
expect our dream to shine along their ways.

But speak the word ! and o'er the adoring whole
straight from the marge of the perfected hours
sudden, large music through the vast, shall roll
a sea of light foaming with seedless flowers;

lilies that form on some ethereal wave,
still generate of the most ancient blue,
burst roses, rootless, knowing not the grave
nor yet the charnel thought by which they grew.

So we shall move at last, untortured powers,
and in white silence hear, as souls unborn,
our hymn given back by the eternal hours
singing together in the eternal morn

1895

I saw my life as whitest flame
light-leaping in a crystal sky,
and virgin colour where it came
pass'd to its heart, in love to die.

It wrapped the world in tender harm
rose-flower'd with one ecstatic pang::
God walk'd amid the hush'd alarm,
and all the trembling region rang

music, whose silver veils dispart
around the carven silences
Memnonian in the hidden heart –
now blithe, effulgurant majesties.

1897

memory droops among the trees
and grasses ponder a vanished trace :
the dream that wanders on the breeze
wafts incense towards a hidden face.

Where the poppy-banners flow
in and out amongst the corn,
spotless morn
ever saw us come and go

hand in hand, as girl and boy
warming fast to youth and maid,
half-afraid
at the hint of passionate joy

hid in summer's rose unblown :
yet we heard nor knew a fear,
strong and clear,
summer's eager clarion blown,

from the sunrise to the set:
now our feet are far away,
night and day,
do the old known spots forget??

Sweet, I wonder if those hours
breathe of us now parted thence,
if a sense
of our love-birth thrill their flowers :

poppies flush all tremulous ;
has our love grown into them,
root and stem,
are the red blooms red with us ?

Summer's banner is unroll'd ;
other lovers wander slow ;
          I would know
if the morn is that of old.

Here our days bloom fuller yet,
and our love is all our task ;
          still I ask :
can those olden days forget??

Deep mists of longing blur the land
as in your late October eve :
almost I think your hand might leave
its old caress upon my hand –

for sure this floating world of dream
hath touch'd that far reality
of memory's heaven; nor would I deem
the chance a strange one, if to thee

my feet should stray ere fall the night,
or, reaching to that lucent shore,
these eyes should wake on tenderer light
to greet the spring and thee once more.

1895

When Summer comes in her glory and brave the whole earth blows,
when colours burn and perfumes impassion the gladden'd air,
then methinks thy laughter seeks me on every breeze that goes
and I feel thy breathing warmth about me everywhere.

Or in the dreamy eve, when our soul is spread in the skies,
when Life for an hour is hush'd, and the gaze is wide to behold
what day may not show nor night, then sure it were no surprise
to find thee beside me sitting, the pitying eyes of old.

But ah, when the winter rains drive hard on the blacken'd pane
and the grief of the lonely wind is lost in the waste outside,
when the room is high and chill and I seek my place in vain,
I know that seas plash cold in the night and the world is wide.

1895

And shall the living waters heed
our vain desire, insensate Art !
and fill the common dust I knead
upgather'd from the trodden mart ?

As well might they forsake their clime
of virgin green and blue, to creep
in cities where our tears are slime,
where our unquicken'd bodies sleep.

– But thou, 0 soul, hast stood for sure
in the far paradisal bower,
there where our passion sparkles pure
beneath the eternal morning hour.

And oft, in twilights listening,
my sleeping memories are stirr'd
by lavings of the unstaunched spring
upwelling in a sudden word.

Why shouldst thou come to squander here
the treasure of those deeps on me ?
nay, where our fount is free and clear
stay there, and let me come to thee !

1895

And does she still perceive, her curtain drawn,
white fields, where maiden Dawn
is anguish'd with the untold approach of joy ?
or in the wooing forenoon softly pass
where of our little friends
that knew us, girl and boy,
the delicate feather-pinks, each dainty greeting bends
before her step, amid the pale sweet grass ?
or warmer flush
our poppies with her blush
as the long day of love grows bold for the red kiss
and dreams of bliss
dizzy the brain and awe the youthful blood ?
Surely her longing gaze hath call'd them forth
the bashful blue-eyed flower-births of the North,
forget-me-nots and violets of the wood,
those maids that slept beneath the snow, and every gracious thing
that glads the spring !
– Ah sweet ! but dream me in thy landscape there
as I have pictured thee
and I shall rest the long day at thy knee
beneath thy hair :
and Thou and I unconscious of surprise
but innocently quiet and gravely glad
and just a little sad
with longing long repress'd,
shall fill with grace each other's welcome eyes
till the shy evening rise
and the streaming lilac-bloom enchant the drowsed air,
hushing it soft and warm round pillows press'd
by happy lovers' rest
lost in that timeless hour when breast is joined to breast.

1895

Of old, on her terrace at evening
– not here – in some long-gone kingdom
oh, folded close to her breast !

Our gaze dwelt wide on the blackness
(was it trees? or a shadowy passion
the pain of an old-world longing
that it sobb'd, that it swell'd, that it shrank?)
– the gloom of the forest
blurr'd soft on the skirt of the night-skies
that shut in our lonely world.
Not here-in some long-gone world ...

Close-lock'd in that passionate arm-clasp
no word did we utter, we stirr'd not :
the silence of Death, or of Love.
Only, round and over us,
that tearless infinite yearning,
and the Night with her spread wings rustling,
folding us with the stars.

Not here – in some long-gone kingdom
of old, on her terrace at evening,
oh, folded close to her heart !

1896

Was it the sun that broke my dream
or was't the dazzle of thy hair
caught where our olden meadows seem
themselves again and yet more fair?

Ah, sun that woke me, limpid stream,
then in spring-mornings' rapture of air !
Was it the sun that broke my dream
or was't the dazzle of thy hair ?

And didst not thou beside me gleam,
brought hither by a tender care
at least my slumbering grief to share ?
Are only the cold seas supreme ?
Was it the sun that broke my dream ?

1896

When the spring mornings grew more long
early I woke from dream that told
of dreaded parting and the cold
of the gray dawns when I should long

to see once more that clear light fall
upon my hands and know that near
the yellow meadows shone with dear
small flowers and hear thy laughter fall

– as now I long only to wake
once in that quiet shine of spring
and dream an hour the hour will bring
thy laughing call that bids me wake

1896

An hour's respite; once more the heart may dream :
the thunderwheels of passion thro' the eve,
distantly musical, vaporously agleam,
about myoid pain leave
nought but a soft enchantment, vesper fable.

Sweet hour of dream ! from the tense height of life
given back to this dear grass and perfumed shade,
across the golden darkness
I feel the simple flowerets where we stray'd
in the clear eves unmix'd with starry strife.

Ah! wilt thou not even now arise,
low-laughing child haunting myoid spring ways
and blossom freshly on my freshen'd gaze,
sororal in this hour of tenderness,
an hour of happy hands and clinging eyes –
on silent heartstrings
sweet memory fades in sweet forgetfulness.

1897

Spring-ripple of green along the way,
keen plash of aery waves that play,
and in my heart
thy dreamy smart, 0 distant day !

Oh whisper hidden in the spring
of days when soul and song took wing
beneath her eyes,
twin smiling skies bent listening.

Oh cruel spell the season weaves !
heart-piercing smell of smoky eves,
all, all is old !
ironic gold that but deceives !

Strange spring, wilt only make me mourn ?
Ah, for thy grace is overworn !
we are the ghost
of spring-tides lost and singing morn !

1897

I am shut out of mine own heart
because my love is far from me,
nor in the wonders have I part
that fill its hidden empery :

the wild wood of adventurous thought
and lands of dawn my dream had won,
the riches out of Faery brought
are buried with our bridal sun.

And I am in a narrow place,
and all its little streets are cold,
because the absence of her face
has robb'd the sullen air of gold.

My home is in a broader day :
at times I catch it glistening
thro' the dull gate, a flower'd play
and odour of undying spring :

the long days that I lived alone,
sweet madness of the springs I miss'd,
are shed beyond, and thro' them blown
clear laughter, and my lips are kiss'd:

– and here, from mine own joy apart,
I wait the turning of the key : –
I am shut out of mine own heart
because my love is far from me.

1897

Spring breezes over the blue,
now lightly frolicking in some tropic bay,
go forth to meet her way,
for here the spell hath won and dream is true.

o happy wind, thou that in her warm hair
mayst rest and play !
could I but breathe all longing into thee,
so were thy viewless wing
as flame or thought, hastening her shining way.

And now I bid thee bring
tenderly hither over a subject sea
that golden one whose grace hath made me king,
and, soon to glad my gaze at shut of day,
loosen'd in happy air
her charmed hair.

1897

White dawn, that tak'st the heaven with sweet surprise
of amorous artifice,
art thou the bearer of my perfect hour
divine, untrod,
from some forgotten window of Paradise
by mighty winds of God
blown down the world, before my haunted eyes
at length to flower ?
Nay, virgin dawn, yet art thou all too known,
too crowded light
to take my boundless hour of flaming peace :
thou common dayspring cease ;
and be there only night, the only night,
more than all other lone :
be the sole secret world
one rose unfurl'd,
and nought disturb its blossom'd peace intense,
that fills the living deep beyond all dreams of sense
enmesh'd in errorous multiplicity :
– let be
nought but her coming there :
what else were fair ?
It asks no golden web, no censer-fire
to tell the dense incarnate mystery
where one delight is wed with one desire.
No leaves bestrow
that passage to the rose of all fulfill'd delight ;
no silver trumpets blow
majestic rite,
but silence that is sigh'd from faery lands,
or wraps the feet of Beauty where she treads
dim fields of fading stars,
be round our meeting heads, and seeking hands :

draw near, ye heavens, and be our chamber-bars ;
and thou, maternal heart of holy night,
close watch, what hush'd and sacramental tide
a soul goes forth wide-eyed,
to meet the archangel-sword of loneliest delight

1897

Four springtimes lost : and in the fifth we stand,
here in this quiet hour of glory, still,
while o'er the bridal land
the westering sun dwells in untroubled gold,
a bridegroom proud of his permitted will,
whom grateful rapture suffers not be bold,
but tender now and bland
his amber locks and bended gaze are shed,
brimming, above the couch'd and happy clime :
all is content and ripe delight, full-fed.
And as your fingers brush my hand
so too the winning time
would charm me from regretful reverie
that keeps me somewhat sad, remembering –
¬not the old woodland days, for thou art near
and hold'st them safely hid
to rise and shine again, when waning skies shall bid –
but later dawns o' the year, away from thee
liv'd thro', even here,
and golden embraces of the light-hearted time
when I was sad at heart, remembering
the clear enchantments of our single year,
our woodland prime of love, its violet-budded vow,
receding ever now
farther and farther down the past, a gleam
that turns to softest pearl the luminous haze
drifting between in from the golden days
when I was sad at inmost heart, remembering
thee and the woodland season of bright laughter: –
so in my perverse and most loitering dream
(0 fading, fading days !)
each season claims the homage due, long after
its glory has faded to an outcast thing.

1898

Old wonder flush'd the east anew
and shed the golden air, and wing
of song that summon'd, from the dew
and rapture of the fields of spring,

old wonder blossom'd in my heart :
because the threatening dream of old,
that nightly wont to bid us part,
now changing, gave me to behold

thy rosy maidenhood that pass'd
and greeted me with stranger grace,
who knew that meeting for our last
and far from mine thy biding-place.

And I have thank'd the threat of sleep,
because the secret heart that flow'd
with phantom wound was proven to keep
beneath its living springs bestow'd

the pang that seven years since was felt
keen thro' my life yet soft dispersed
along all veins that thrill or melt-
old wonder, blossom'd, not in hears'd :

and eyes perchance made dull and slow
by the long days' subtle dusty mesh
waked gladly from their fear, to know
old wonder, old and ever fresh.

1900

The winter eve is clear and chill :
the world of air is folded still ;
the quiet hour expects the moon ;
and yon my home awaits me soon
behind the panes that come and go
with dusk and firelight wavering low :
and I must bid the prompting cease
that bids me, in this charmed peace,
– as tho' the hour would last my will –
follow the roads and follow still
the dream that holds my heart in trance
and lures it to the fabled chance
to find, beyond these evening ways,
the morning and the woodland days
and meadows clear with gold, and you
as once, ere I might dare to woo.

1906

Christopher Brennan, a portrait by May Moore.

APPENDIX

Stéphane Mallarmé, a portrait by Nadar, Paris, 1890.

D.M.
STÉPHANE MALLARMÉ
DEAD IN VALVINS
9. IX. 1898

Red autumn in Valvins around thy bed
was watchful flame or yet thy spirit induced
might vanish away in magic gold diffused
and kingdom o'er the dreaming forest shed.

What god now claims thee priest, O chosen head,
most humble here that wast, for that thou knew'st
thro' what waste nights thy lucid gaze was used
to spell our glory in blazon'd ether spread ?

Silence alone, that o'er the lonely song
impends, old night, or, known to thee and near,
long autumn afternoon o'er stirless leaves

suspended fulgent haze, the smouldering throng
staying its rapt assumption-pyre to hear
what strain the faun's enamour'd leisure weaves.

Stéphane Mallarmé, an etching by Paul Gauguin, 1891.

LETTERS BETWEEN MALLARMÉ AND BRENNAN

Mallarmé to Brennan

Paris 89 rue de Rome, [Tuesday] 9 January [1894]

Dear Sir,

I am flattered by the interest you are taking in my published works. No, I do not reserve the right to sell or distribute any of them. Not even the photo-engraved edition of my poetry (the current edition is still just about to come out [*be published*] in Belgium:) the large, luxury [*de luxe*] reproduction of my manuscript in question, was limited to 40 copies which are at present scattered far and wide or reappear at book-sales, at about their original price of one hundred francs. I have only my own copy at my place. A list of my works, which I have had written out [copied] for you, is enclosed with this card and will answer all your queries.

Believe me, dear Sir, yours very truly

Stéphane Mallarmé

Brennan to Mallarmé

Public Library, Sydney, 3rd October 1896.

Dear Sir,

Our friend Mr. Weymark has delivered to me your notice of Madame Morisot – which, in effect, it would have been difficult for me to obtain – enriched, for me, personally, by the fact that it came, signed, from your hand and the kind expressions of your letter. Nor did I any less eagerly receive the news of the approaching reappearance of your poems.

I pray you to believe in the sincere gratitude for your gift (not merely the printed pages) which this letter endeavours to express, but which still remains a debt – a part of that larger debt of gratitude (may I be permitted to make allusion to it?) which I, with some others, must ever owe you.

Believe me, Sir,
most respectfully and
cordially yours,
Chris: Brennan.

Brennan to Mallarmé

Dear Sir,

For the graciousness which you manifested to me, a stranger, I may never make fitting return: & perhaps this sending will only show you that your kindness has embolden'd me to disturb you with my presence. But I also feel that this little book of verse is due to you & thro' you, to the literature of your race. It was appointed that I should use a language which must seem foreign to me; that I should be almost entirely cut off from the legendary tradition of my Celtic ancestors: &, as many an Irishman in other days found a new home in France, so I have found in her literature a spirit, in her writers a style, to which I feel myself instinctively drawn, as some are drawn towards home. In sending you this slight book, Sir, I would, if I might, at least mark my gratitude – to you, especially, as the poet whose works have been to me the greatest renewal, the greatest revelation.

If my verse fails of being the homage I had intended, at least regard me, Sir, as the most faithful of your readers – that pride I shall always guard.

I am, Sir,
most respectfully &
most sincerely yours,
Chris: Brennan.

Public Library, Sydney, NSW August 9th 1897.

Mallarmé to Brennan

Valvins, near Fontainebleau [Thursday] 16 September 1897

My dear Brennan,

Addressing you thus, instead of Poet, wonderful Poet – yes, indeed, this heartfelt, delighted greeting intimates [*implies*] everything or that there is between you and me some dreamworld affinity [*kinship*]; thank you for the charming, personal copy that you have bound especially for me, impressing on it, in advance, as a seal upon a book, placed in my library within easy reach, my monogram. *Towards the source* is no empty [*idle*] title: you move [*surge*] back wildly, powerfully, limpidly, up the everyday current of poetry towards its rarest source. Words, choice words, you use just inasmuch as they are needed – tempered, purified in what primordial life-stream, bathed in [*amidst*] essential inspiration. Yes, indeed, although its language is totally English, I can truly sense that your song has passed through our own: but it gives one the feeling, too, that such it would have been [... *that it would have been as it now is*], through itself and by itself alone.

Thank you, as a reader or, since this name is, from afar, dear to you,

Stéphane Mallarmé

Brennan to Mallarmé

Public Library, Sydney, NSW 2nd January 1898.

My dear Sir,

– This formal address I had gladly suppressed, if only to leave a blank; how can I respond to your friendly greeting? –

Shall I have your pardon for my long delay in sending you thanks? excessive work, only just brought to an end, and my recent marriage involving much care before-hand, may perhaps excuse me.

Let me here thank you heartily for the words you have sent me, an encouragement to further effort – a joy, as showing that you hold me worthy, at this distance and unseen, of your friendship.

Most respectfully &
most heartily yours
Chris: Brennan.

POEMS IN *XXI POEMS*

FIRST NOCTURN (*Northern*)

..in locum refrigerii ..

I will free my soul from this stifling place,
I will plunge where the waters are cold and roar !
I will dash myself into the midst of their race:
Below in the forest I know the place –
The woods hide the dam over which they pour,
But I hear them ever in the lonely night –
And there where the whiten'd wave
Strains back towards the peace forsaken – repentant,
in vain ! – I will plunge and lave
My naked body, my throbbing soul
That the waters may heal and save.

Or hush ! Do you hear ? It sounds like the sea !
Yes, the sea must be near ! it would make me whole :
I will steal me out of the the hothouse at night
When she sees me not, when she heeds not me
When her cruel play hath other prey
I will creep down till the mother's call from the
stifling house – you will not betray ?
Creep down and leap
Headlong into their bosom. The waters ! drink long and deep
Cool me, lave me without and within,
Cool the hotness of mortal sin
Yield up the mortal breath –

O the deep
O the sea-wind's breadth and the blue,
The speaking blue of the mystic night !

They shall freshen my soul from its fever of sleep
From its dream of death
And the flesh shall be born anew !

Then beat me ye waves ! O beat me to death,
Whirl me, buried in your seething spray !
I will none of your languid ironic caresses
Such as she yields here in the night of her tresses –
That fritter the soul away –
Up here in the hothouse : she laughs in the night
When the fever'd desire
May find no delight
In the pleasure withheld till the joy is fled
And the heart grown fierce, till the soul is dead
And passion paler with hate :
But cruel, O sea, will I have you and fierce and strong in your changing ire
To drown this passion, to quench this fire
That is eating my soul away.

(Is it not too late ?)

Then cleans'd might I walk in my mists again
That my soul loves, haunted by loves without stain
Pallid as the mists and cold as they
That I dream of ever in the lonely night –
O their silver silence, the mists ! lo, there
They dream over river-bank and lake!
Thro' the hothouse glass I see them wake
To the lamp of the rising moon : – my prayer
Dost thou hear it, Lord ? do I cry in vain ?
Is there no way out of the choking air ?

SECOND NOCTURN (*Tropic*)

Sighing –
the wind from the equator thro' the trees
faintly fell
or wander'd like a spirit ill at ease,
that we heard its echoes dying
where we lay
in our chamber by the tropic ocean's swell
night and day.
Lying –
side by side –
we heard the rising ocean to the dying wind replying,
heard its surge advance with still insistent call
or subside
to the night-wind's dying fall
sighing –
thro' the night we heard it sobbing
as the tide
rose in rhythmic monotone;
till at last our twin hearts pulsed upon ita ceaseless throbbing,
till we felt them fall and rise and drift asunder
leagues of night between them thrown –
O so wide !
O the wonder
that we felt but a vague and strange emotion
felt a dim and blind and infinite emotion
of the mystery, the wonder
that the night-wind and the ocean
and the traitor night should set us twain asunder

who were lying,
heart to heart,
in our love-chamber by the boundless ocean –
there were lying –
yet apart,
sunder'd by the nightly ocean
heart from heart !

BELLS

.. paco cruentos ..

After the garish day
its dust and turbulence and aching glare,
fled to familiar night
I sat at the evening's quiet work
freshen'd in brain and nerve ;
paused for a moment in the quiet labour
– the golden lamplight brooded on the floor
and all seem'd to listen to the churchbells ringing
solemn and glad, across the lake of memory,
a far-off strain of peace :
Peace !
no craving, no unrest ..
seeing all, hearing all,
giving thanks ever,
not of the world but dwelling in it
cloister'd, watchers of eternity
chant we the hours
untouch'd by the day or its glare !
but at monastic midnight
sing we for him that will hear us
faithful ever, our hymn of praise
content in the peace of our dream.

AUBADE

We woke together on a gusty dawn
in the dim house amid the level waste
and stared in anguish on the stretch of years
fill'd with grey dawn and ever-weeping wind

for as the hour hung still ’twixt night and day
we whom the dark had drawn so close together
at that dead tide as strangers saw each other
strangers divided by a sea of years

we might not weep out our passion of despair
but in lorn trance we gazed upon each other
and wonder’d what strange ways had brought our hands
together in that chamber of the west

we felt the dumb compulsion of the hour
to wander forth in spirit on the wind
and drift far apart in undiscover’d realms
of some blank world where dawn for ever wept

(FATUM)

Dumb Sibyl, sitting at my birth
(or shall I call thee Sphinx?) that thought
My riddle thus in brain distraught
.. *His Elsinore the patient earth,*
this shivering loon shall drape himself
among congenial rocks and daws
play Hamlet to his soul's applause
and pay him with his fancy's pelf ..

unseal thy lips if ne'er again !
and if I may not swing me high
where nuptial-songs of sea and sky
might fit my soul for Imogen

teach me at least of such desires
to lay the ghost and so escape
scorn of the night my trappings ape
and keen derision of its fires.

David Brooks is currently an Honorary Associate Professor at the University of Sydney, where he taught Australian Literature from 1991 until 2013. From 2000 until 2018 he was also co-editor of the journal *Southerly*. A poet and writer of fiction, he received, in 2025, both the Prime Minister's Award for Poetry, and the Patrick White Award. He has written many essays and articles on nineteenth- and twentieth-century Australian poetry and is the author of *The Sons of Clovis: Ern Malley, Adoré Floupette, and a Secret History of Australian Poetry*, and *Animal Dreams* (essays on non-human animals in contemporary philosophy and literature, mainly Australian).

www.ingramcontent.com/pod-product-compliance
Lightning Source LLC
LaVergne TN
LVHW052348100826
845147LV00012B/786

* 9 7 8 1 9 2 3 5 2 7 2 2 5 *